YOUR KNOWLEDGE HAS VALUE

- We will publish your bachelor's and master's thesis, essays and papers

- Your own eBook and book - sold worldwide in all relevant shops

- Earn money with each sale

Upload your text at www.GRIN.com
and publish for free

Bibliographic information published by the German National Library:

The German National Library lists this publication in the National Bibliography; detailed bibliographic data are available on the Internet at http://dnb.dnb.de .

This book is copyright material and must not be copied, reproduced, transferred, distributed, leased, licensed or publicly performed or used in any way except as specifically permitted in writing by the publishers, as allowed under the terms and conditions under which it was purchased or as strictly permitted by applicable copyright law. Any unauthorized distribution or use of this text may be a direct infringement of the author s and publisher s rights and those responsible may be liable in law accordingly.

Imprint:

Copyright © 2012 GRIN Verlag
Print and binding: Books on Demand GmbH, Norderstedt Germany
ISBN: 9783668619265

This book at GRIN:

https://www.grin.com/document/388006

Marco Schmidbauer

The Search for Identity in "The Buddha of Suburbia" by Hanif Kureishi

GRIN Verlag

GRIN - Your knowledge has value

Since its foundation in 1998, GRIN has specialized in publishing academic texts by students, college teachers and other academics as e-book and printed book. The website www.grin.com is an ideal platform for presenting term papers, final papers, scientific essays, dissertations and specialist books.

Visit us on the internet:

http://www.grin.com/

http://www.facebook.com/grincom

http://www.twitter.com/grin_com

University of Regensburg

Faculty of Humanities

English & American Studies

Seminar: PS English Literature III

SoSe 2012

The Buddha of Suburbia: Search for Identity

by Marco Schmidbauer

Term Paper

The Buddha of Suburbia: Search for Identity

"My name is Karim Amir, and I am an Englishman born and bred, almost" (BS 3). The beginning of the novel already reveals the struggle for identity. But what exactly is identity? No one can give a clear definition on what it is - we can only limit the factors that determine identity, such as class, gender, sexual preference, ethnic background and education. Moreover, identity is bound to social norms. A boy for example is expected to like football or cars, whereas girls are expected to be interested in fashion and shoes. If a person fails to fulfill his gender role, he/she is automatically seen as different and not normal. This way stereotypes are formed. Stereotypes are fixed notions of racial identities, developed over the years. Even though often unconsciously: every person generalizes - this is just how the human mind works. When we see a person for the first time, we immediately tend to put the other into certain categories. Fortunately, identity is not fixed but a malleable entity constructed through social performance. Social performance includes your way of clothing, behavior, accent and much more. In general, it is your outer appearance combined with your gestures and facial expressions, as well as your way of speaking. To my mind, every single person creates its own identity unconsciously. On top of that, nobody can judge his identity by himself - it is judged by others. Every step you take, and every single reaction of yours in certain situations merge your identity. It is how other people see and perceive you, while you are yourself. If you try to be someone you are not, it falsifies your identity and people are not able to see your true self. However, every person struggles to find his true identity himself. The people in *The Buddha of Suburbia* have a hard time finding it, which leads me to the topic of my paper: the search for identity. I will go into detail about the characters that define their identity through their social performance, like Charlie with his different music genres and fashion styles; Haroon and his role of the Buddha through exotic clothing and customs; and Karim with his problems of finding himself because of self-perception and stereotypes of others. Every single one of them approaches this struggle differently. These 3 characters impersonate Hanif Kureishi's representation and creation of identity through performance and overthrow the idea of the authentic.

Charlie Kay, or later on called "Charlie Hero", is Eva's son and Karim's role model. He is a handsome guy, easy-going and very ambitious when it comes to pursuing his dreams. Charlie is one of the characters, who know exactly what they want right from the start. To make his dream of becoming a rockstar come true, he is willing to give up his whole identity and start a new one from scratch. He is not afraid of doing anything to achieve his aims and changes his character to appeal to his audience by using different music genres and fashion styles to reinvent himself several times throughout the story. One time, he "reinvents himself as a Ziggy Stardust-like 'spaceman' with 'short, spiky hair dyed white' as well as 'silver shoes and a shiny silver jacket' " (Buchanan 45, BS 35/37). Another day he joins Karim to a bar called "Nashville", where Charlie gets to know the members of a punk band by jumping into their car after their show, of which he is very impressed: "That's it, that's it (...)The sixties have been given notice tonight. Those kids we saw have assassinated all hope. They're the fucking future" (BS 131). Even though Charlie hates the way the punk band in the club behaves and judges their instruments as "unprofessional" (BS 130), he is still willing to adapt their style in order to succeed. When Karim dismisses his behaviour as artificial, stating that they are not like them, and they have not been through what they (the Punks) been through, Charlie suddenly gets very angry: "You're not going anywhere, Karim. You're not doing anything with your life because as usual you're facing in the wrong direction and going the wrong way" (BS 132). Charlie is so adamant to succeed that it does not matter to him to adapt to fashion styles and music he does not like. Later on in the story, Charlie eventually becomes very famous, so he goes to New York to make the most profit out of it. Having arrived in the USA, he uses a fake cockney accent in order to sell his Englishness (BS 247). Moreover, Charlie changes his style of music and fashion again: the ferocity of the punk sound is gone, making way for a more feeble and dull sound; he wears black leather clothes with chains and chokers and appeals now to a far different audience like gays and young girls (BS 247).

However, it should not be forgotten that fame and success comes with its price. Charlie suffers from sudden blowups of temper. When he and Karim go out for dinner in a restaurant, he feels observed: "Why are people staring at me when I'm trying to eat my food! That woman with the powder puff on her head, she can fuck off" (BS 251)! Another day he beats up a persistent journalist, who wants to interview him: "Charlie chopped down on him, but the man held on. Charlie hit him with a playground punch on the side of the head, and the man went down, stunned, on to his knees, waving his arms like someone begging forgiveness" (BS 252). These examples show that the fame went to Charlie's head and that not everything in his life is peace, love and harmony. Moreover, taking into account the beginning of the story, Charlie was like a role-model for Karim and Karim was happy to be in his presence. In the end of the novel it appears to be exactly the other way around. Charlie now depends on Karim because his success and fame isolate him from society and actual people he can trust. Moreover, Karim has known him from childhood days and is therefore the only person who could "appreciate how far he'd come from his original state in Beckenham" (BS 250). Charlie does not want Karim to return to London but eventually lets him go (BS 256/257). To conclude, Charlie's character changes as well as his identity. Since Charlie is clearly the most flexible character throughout the story, he proves that identity is certainly not fixed but constructed through social performance.

The next character with an identity defined through performance is Haroon, the namesake of the novel. Haroon is Karim's father and is given many nicknames throughout the narrative, including: "God," "Harry," "Daddio" and "Buddha". He is a first generation immigrant from India and stuck in a job he hates and an unhappy marriage. This is why he begins a relationship with Eva Kay because she - in contrast to his wife - shares his interest in Buddhism and Eastern Philosophy. She encourages Haroon to share his outlook with others, so he starts holding meditation and yoga sessions in the neighborhood. Because of his looks and behavior everyone believes in his wisdom but since Haroon is only "a renegade Muslim masquerading as a Buddhist" (BS 16) the cultural authenticity gets lost. Furthermore, "the novel pokes fun at the way Haroon discovers and cultivates his Otherness (from 'books on Buddhism, Sufism, Confucianism and Zen which he had bought at the Oriental bookshop') and stages it to suite white audiences, *after* coming to Britain (BS 5)" (Ranasinha 69). Eva herself sees Haroon as the embodiment of eastern spirituality and Helen, a girlfriend of Karim, also shares this taste for exoticism: "We like you being here. You benefit our country with your traditions" (BS 74). In order to make his performance more authentic, Haroon even tries to relearn his old Indian accent by "hissing his s's" (BS 21) and wearing exotic clothes. Moreover, Haroon has to practice his performance to play "the Buddha" more convincingly. This artificial performance reinforces and challenges the stereotypical notion of Indianness. It appears at first that Haroon's behaviour is very similar to Charlie's, but it is not just the fame and success he covets. Haroon earnestly believes in his teachings - in contrast to Charlie. While Charlie does not like any of the music he adapts, Haroon is really convinced of his religion. In addition, Haroon is a very thoughtful character. Even though he is happy with Eva, he seems to regret leaving his wife and feels guilty about it. The main compliance between the two is that Haroon is selling his Indianness, whereas Charlie is selling his Englishness. To conclude, both of them overthrow the idea of the authentic, since both falsify their true selves in order to appeal to a certain audience.

Karim Amir is the protagonist of the novel. He is a very shy person without self-confidence, who hasn't got many friends. As the beginning of the novel already suggests ("Englishman born and bred, almost" BS 3), he is a mixed-race teenager, with an Indian father and an English mother. Because of this dual heritage, Karim is always caught in between his Indianness and Englishness, leading to a confusion on his side of where to belong. Beyond that, Karim's ethnicity is not the only sphere, where he is caught up in between: his sexual orientation is also complicated. Throughout the story Karim has many sexual relationships, some with men, some with women. Since Karim does not claim to be homosexual/heterosexual or Indian/English he always has to negotiate between either one: "I was looking for trouble, any kind of movement, action and sexual interest I could find, because things were so gloomy, so slow and heavy, in our family, I don't know why" (BS 3). On top of that, Karim feels an opposition between societal conceptions of his identity and his self-perception which often leads him to a state of desperation as the novel progresses. The start of his career as an actor already marks such an opposition. Eva's old friend Jeremy Shadwell offers him a role as Mowgli in *The Jungle Book*. At first, Karim is really passionate and happy about it but it turns out that Shadwell only chose him because of his exotic looks: "Karim, you have been cast for authenticity and not for experience" (BS 147).

Shadwell forces Karim to speak in an Indian accent in order to make the play more authentic. Moreover, Karim has to wear loin-cloth and brown make up on his skin to improve his looks (BS 146). Later on, Karim joins the theatre group of a man called Matthew Pyke, where he is confronted with similar problems. When the actors are asked to improvise characters, Karim initially chooses Charlie but is immediately discourages by Pyke: "We need someone from your own background (...) Someone black" (BS 170). Eager to please his director, Karim rushes off to study Anwar and plays him in front of the group afterwards - but gets mixed reactions. Tracey, the only black actress in the group feels offended and worried about how Karim depicts minorities because she is directly affected: "Anwar's hunger strike worries me. What you want to say hurts me (...) I'm afraid it shows black people (...) As being irrational, ridiculous, as being hysterical. And as being fanatical" (BS 180). Furthermore, she goes on that Karim shows minority groups as "unorganized aggressors" (BS 180), which is the worst thing to do because they have to protect their culture these days (BS 181). As Susanne Reichl puts it, Karim "cannot see why he should identify as black - "I didn't know anyone black" (BS 170) - and entirely misses her point of him representing a minority group" (Reichl 146). Leaving out information on the arranged marriage for example would mean censorship to him. This dialogue between Tracey and Karim highlights that the issue of identity is also closely linked with issues of representation (Reichl 146). As Pyke suggests that Karim may have to rethink his character Anwar, he invents a figure named Tariq based on Changez. From now on, Karim gets very ambitious. He keeps a journal to note down his thoughts and notions in order to become a better actor. Being the creator of this character makes him feel "more solid myself" (BS 217). Alongside, Pyke guides him on his way of becoming a successful actor, explaining the "paradox of acting": "when in character, playing not-me, you have to be yourself. To make your not-self real you have to steal from your authentic self (...) to be someone else successfully you must be yourself" (BS 219/220).

As Susie Thomas puts it, "Kureishi suggests that posing can be a rehearsal for the real thing" (Thomas 66). In other words, by representing someone else, one is able to learn and make a profit from it, which comes in handy for your own life. Mentioned before, Karim is a mixed-race teenager but it seems that by becoming a successful actor, he identifies himself more and more with the western culture and somehow denies his Indian roots. This notion changes with the funeral of his uncle Anwar. Karim looks around the Indian people and begins to realize his heritage: "But I did feel, looking at these strange creatures now– the Indians – that in some way these were my people, and that I'd spent my life denying or avoiding that fact" (BS 212). Another important point concerning his identity linked with his performance as an actor is the feedback he receives from his next of kin. His mother thinks the idea of him playing an Indian is ridiculous (Reichl 144). She sees him more as an Englishman since he has never even been to India: "At least they let you wear your own clothes. But you're not an Indian. You've never been to India. You'd get diarrhoea the minute you stepped off that plane, I know you would" (BS 232). On top of that, as Susanne Reichl states that "even though he seems to be happy constructing his Indian identity on stage, he is not altogether at home with himself" (Reichl 144). Moreover, it seems that Karim is never completely satisfied throughout the story, which could be an ongoing result of his struggle for identity and recognition. He is not happy with school, his role in *The Jungle Book* or his role as Tariq. It seems that Karim always has to "act" his identity in order to fulfill other people's expectations of him as the "exotic other". Also, Karim's problematic sexual relationships trigger his displeasure. His bisexuality reveals another side of him where he is not quite sure of where to belong. The first chapter of the novel suggests that Karim has no clear sexual preference and will sleep with anyone, male or female: "I was looking for trouble, any kind of movement, action and sexual interest I could find" (BS 3). His following sexual experiences range from early encounters with Charlie and Helen to a regular relationship with Jamila, a cousin of him. Jamila's father Anwar forces her into an arranged marriage, which makes her feel very lonely. Therefore, she seeks Karim's company and they often engage in casual sex with each other. Nevertheless, their sex and relationship has never an emotional component but is more about satisfying their sex drives. Later on, as Karim gets involved in Pyke's theatre group in New York, he begins a complicated relationship with an actress called Eleanor. Karim has serious feelings for her and describes their relationship, saying, "I'd never had such a strong emotional and physical feeling before" (BS 187). For the first time in his life, Karim is truly in love: "I couldn't stop kissing her face. I just wanted to hold her all day and stroke her, tickle her, play with her" (BS 196).

Unfortunately, their relationship does not last very long, since Eleanor feels attracted to Pyke and trusts him more than she trusts Karim: "You don't understand other people. It would be dangerous for me to lay myself open to you" (BS 198). Furthermore, she regularly has sex with Pyke, which leads to Karim leaving her. However, Karim gains some interesting insights, when he discovers one of Eleanor's secrets. Eleanor's dead boyfriend Gene was also an actor with Indian heritage but even though being really talented, "he never got the work he deserved" (BS 201). Gene was offered only minor roles, depicting him as a stereotypical alien. Furthermore, he had several encounters of racism, because "taxis drove straight past him" and there were "no free tables in empty restaurants" (BS 201) for him. One day, he committed suicide because he could not take it any longer: "Sweet Gene, her black lover (...) killed himself because every day, by a look, a remark, an attitude the English told him they hated him; they never let him forget they thought him a nigger, a slave, a lower being" (BS 227). Karim now sees the crudeness and brutality of the actor business and faces the consequences of Gene's death. If he is not able to "find his own role to play in British society, whether onstage or off, he too is doomed" (Buchanan 50). As the show of Pyke gets cancelled, Karim goes back to London and gets offered a job in a soap opera, which is - again - an ethnic role. Karim should play the rebellious son of an Indian shopkeeper but he is really passionate about it: "I was being given a part in a new soap opera which would tangle with the latest contemporary issues: they meant abortions and racist attacks, the stuff that people lived through but that never got on TV" (BS 259). In this case, Karim is happy because he finally gets to play a role - although being an ethnic one again - which portrays the cruel and racist environment foreigners have to live in. Here, the Indians are not displayed as bad and fanatic people but as victims of society. Furthermore, Karim would earn a lot of money through that show. In the end, Karim is happy to be back at home with the people he loves and the book leaves the reader with a confident glimpse of the future: "I thought of what a mess everything had been, but that it wouldn't always be that way" (BS 284). Together, one can say that Karim is a very indecisive young man, who needs much time to develop and realize what things matter the most in life. Because of social constraints he is always expected to fulfill his role as an actor as the "exotic other," which limit his horizon but also make him gain important insights into his own psyche and heritage. His performances lead Karim to greater self knowledge and the numerous encounters of racism, ethnicity and sexuality make him grow on his journey to become a successful and upright person.

As we have seen, there are several ways to redefine your identity through social performance. These three characters have come a long way from the beginning to the end of the novel and it is crucial to see that a performed identity is not restricted to black characters or postcolonial issues (Reichl 145), since Charlie is a white person. Moreover, "the fact that all characters in question have a job in which they perform - Karim is an actor, Charlie a singer, Haroon teaches mysticism, Eva creates houses like stages - doubles the importance of the act and erases any clear borders between private and public, authentic and assumed, real and fake" (Reichl 145). To come back to my own opinion of identity - your own identity is how other people judge you, when you are yourself - Karim has grown the most out of the three. From being shy, indecisive and unambitious he has become a much more straightforward and determined guy. Throughout the story he never deviated from his opinions and always spoke what he had in mind without lying. Therefore, Karim has a bright future in front of him. Charlie on the other hand - even though, having succeeded in becoming a famous rockstar - does not reach total fulfillment. Also, his treatment of other characters and their decisions highlight his unstable personality. Because of his changing fashion and music styles people never see his true identity beyond the surface. Therefore, Charlie will never be able to be seen as the person he is in reality. On the second hand we have Haroon, who seems not entirely happy at the end as well. Although having pursued his dreams of becoming a guru, he sometimes seems to regret his decision of leaving his wife. He finally starts to realize that the divorce is irrevocable and things will never be the same again. Even though he has found his match in Eva, she does not seem to realize that Haroon is not 100% happy.

Works cited

Buchanan, Bradley. *Hanif Kureishi*. Basingstoke, Hampshire: Palgrave Macmillan, 2007. Print.

Kureishi, Hanif. *The Buddha of Suburbia*. London: Faber and Faber, 1999. Print.

Ranasinha, Ruvani. *Hanif Kureishi*. Tavistock: Northcote House, 2002. Print.

Reichl, Susanne. "Hanif Kureishi, The Buddha of Suburbia: Performing Identity in Postcolonial London." *A History of Postcolonial Literature in 12 1/2 Books*. Ed. Tobias Döring. Trier: WVT Wissenschaftlicher Verlag Trier, 2007. 139-154. Print.

YOUR KNOWLEDGE HAS VALUE

- We will publish your bachelor's and master's thesis, essays and papers

- Your own eBook and book - sold worldwide in all relevant shops

- Earn money with each sale

Upload your text at www.GRIN.com
and publish for free